Read & Respond

FOR KS2

SECTION 1
The Wreck of the Zanzibar
Teachers' notes 3

SECTION 2
Guided reading
Teachers' notes 4

SECTION 3
Shared reading
Teachers' notes 7
Photocopiable extracts 8

SECTION 4
Plot, character and setting
Activity notes 11
Photocopiable activities 15

SECTION 5
Talk about it
Activity notes 19
Photocopiable activities 22

SECTION 6
Get writing
Activity notes 25
Photocopiable activities 28

SECTION 7
Assessment
Teachers' notes and activities 31
Photocopiable activity 32

Read & Respond

FOR KS2

Author: Campbell Perry

Editor: Frances Ridley

Assistant Editor: Niamh O'Carroll

Series Designer: Anna Oliwa

Designer: Helen Taylor

Cover Image: Christian Birmingham

Illustrations: Jane Bottomley

Text © 2006 Campbell Perry;
© 2006 Scholastic Ltd

Designed using Adobe InDesign

Published by Scholastic Ltd, Villiers House, Clarendon Avenue, Leamington Spa, Warwickshire CV32 5PR
www.scholastic.co.uk

Printed by Bell & Bain
123456789 6789012345

British Library Cataloguing-in-Publication Data
A catalogue record for this book is available from the British Library.
ISBN 0-439-96583-7   ISBN 978-0439-96583-5

The rights of Campbell Perry to be identified as the author of this work have been asserted by him in accordance with the Copyright, Designs and Patents Act 1988.

Extracts from The National Literacy Strategy © Crown copyright. Reproduced under the terms of HMSO Guidance Note 8.

All rights reserved. This book is sold subject to the condition that it shall not, by way of trade or otherwise, be lent, hired out or otherwise circulated without the publisher's prior consent in any form of binding or cover other than that in which it is published and without a similar condition, including this condition, being imposed upon the subsequent purchaser.

No part of this publication may be reproduced, stored in a retrieval system, or transmitted, in any form or by any means, electronic, mechanical, photocopying, recording or otherwise, without the prior permission of the publisher. This book remains copyright, although permission is granted to copy pages where indicated for classroom distribution and use only in the school which has purchased the book, or by the teacher who has purchased the book, and in accordance with the CLA licensing agreement. Photocopying permission is given only for purchasers and not for borrowers of books from any lending service.

Acknowledgements

Jane Bottomley for the reuse of illustrations from *Read and Respond: The Wreck of the Zanzibar* by Angel Scott Illustrations © 1998, Jane Bottomley (1998, Scholastic Ltd.) **Egmont Children's Books** for the use of extracts from *The Wreck of the Zanzibar* by Michael Morpurgo © 1995, Michael Morpurgo (1995, Egmont UK Limited, London). **Random House Group** for the use of an extract from *The Secret Diary of Adrian Mole Aged 13¾* by Sue Townsend © 1982, Sue Townsend (1982, Methuen) **Scholastic Children's Books** for the use of an extract from *Blitz: The Diary of Edie Benson: London 1940-1941* by Vince Cross © 2001, Vince Cross (2001, Scholastic Children's Books).

The Wreck of the Zanzibar

SECTION 1

About the book

The Wreck of the Zanzibar is a story told in the first person by two narrators. This structure gives the story impact, immediacy and fictional authenticity. Michael is the first narrator. He is an adult, returning to his childhood holiday haunt of Bryher to attend his Great-aunt Laura's funeral. Back in her tiny cottage, the memories come flooding back. All her relatives gather together to celebrate her life. Michael is given Laura's diary, which reveals the events of one year, 1907, in the life of her family. It tells of their struggle for survival in an unforgiving climate. Her twin brother Billy runs away to sea, leaving a desolate void in their lives. When a terrible storm wrecks the family's livelihood, Laura's father is about to take them away from Bryher forever. However, just when it seems things could not get any worse, their fortunes change. A shipwreck brings hope for the future and, for Laura, an opportunity to realise a burning ambition.

The diary style makes the account accessible to the reader and very personal. Laura, through her description of family and events, unfolds a story of tragedy and eventual triumph but also reveals her own hopes, dreams and aspirations. Laura's indomitable spirit shines through every page.

The Wreck of the Zanzibar can be used to explore aspects of narrative structure (Year 6 Term 2 T1). It also provides an opportunity to look at stories based on historical events, such as that of Grace Darling, and also other diaries, such as *The Diary of Anne Frank* (factual) and *The Secret Diary of Adrian Mole aged 13¾* (fictional).

About the author

Michael Morpurgo is one of the most successful children's authors in the country. He has written over 100 children's books, some of which have been adapted for film (*Why the Whales Came*) and stage (*Kensuke's Kingdom*). He discovered the magic of story-telling as a teacher. The children he taught were bored by the book he was reading to them, so he told them the kind of stories he told his own children. Although he is no longer a teacher, he is still involved in working with children. In 1976, he and his wife Clare started 'Farms for City Children'. This charity provides an opportunity for children from inner cities to experience life on a farm for one week.

Michael Morpurgo maintains that the idea for a book can come from anywhere. His best advice to budding writers is to be open-minded. In his own words: 'I keep my eyes and ears open, my heart fresh.'

> **Facts and figures**
> Michael Morpurgo was the Children's Laureate from 2003 to 2005.
> *The Wreck of the Zanzibar* won the Whitbread Children's Novel Award in 1995 and has sold over 150,000 copies.

READ & RESPOND: Activities based on The Wreck of the Zanzibar

Guided reading

SECTION 2

'Great-aunt Laura' – February 15th

Read the opening of the book, 'Great-aunt Laura', with the children. Michael has come to his great-aunt's funeral on the tiny island of Bryher. This event provides the 'fictional authenticity' for the story. (The story, the characters and the opening event, that is, Great-aunt Laura's funeral, are fictions. However, funerals in general are a natural event and the setting is a real place.) As the children read the opening, ask them to suggest how the reader is enticed into the story. (Michael's childhood memories, the diary, the letter and the mystery surrounding Zanzibar.) What do they think 'Zanzibar' is?

Read the first diary entry. Can the children suggest why italics are being used for the diary? (It is a means of separating the past from the present.) Ask the children who narrates the story's opening. (Michael.) Who is narrating in the diary entry? (Great-aunt Laura as a child.)

The first three diary entries introduce Laura's 'present' – 1907. She writes as she speaks and gives a great deal of information about herself and her family. Ask the children to find quotes that identify her dreams and hopes. Encourage them to look for references in the text that tell them about Laura's relationship with Billy and Billy's with his father.

Laura describes the coming of the storm. Can the children identify another storm brewing in her life? (The thunderclouds gathering in the life of her family.) The clues to this storm are the behaviour of Billy and the arrival of Joseph Hannibal. Ask the children why they think Laura writes 'This is the worst day of my whole life' at the beginning of the diary entry for February 15th. Why do they think there are no more entries until July 21st? (The loss of Billy, the emptiness in her life.)

July 21st – September 7th

In these diary entries, the aftermath of Billy's departure is made evident by a variety of means. Ask the children how the writer has linked the events in the natural world with the family's feelings. (The relationship between the plight of the family's cattle and the depression within the family.) Ask the children to find evidence in the text which links the two. (Mother sitting rocking on Billy's bed, the cows aren't milking well, the disappointment that Laura feels listening to the vicar, the cows becoming sick, the coming of the storm.)

On July 30th and 31st, Laura talks about hope. Ask the class how she has come to view hope. (As something to be disappointed by.) Laura tries to realise her hopes of rowing in the gig. She asks her father if she can and says: 'I knew I shouldn't but I had to.' Ask the children why she thinks she shouldn't have asked. (Her father is already preoccupied by Billy's departure and now the sickness of the cattle.) Why do they think she did – was it selfish or was it a question of hope? (It was her burning ambition and, when all other hope seemed lost, she needed something to believe in.)

Laura describes the effect Billy's departure has on her parents. Ask the class to look for quotes in the text to show how they feel, and the changing relationship between them.

In the diary entry for July 21st, Laura describes the island as a prison. Ask the children why they think she does this. (Feelings of isolation, no escape.) In the diary entry for September 7th, the storm has passed and the island is devastated. Ask the class to find evidence linking the devastation on the island to the effect the storm has had on the family's livelihood (the drowned cows). Although the storm has wrecked their property, the entry ends with the family beginning to reach out to each other again. Can the children find evidence of this in the text? (Mother and Granny May leading Father home, Father crying, Laura realising that she still loved him, Mother putting her arms round him.)

Ask the children to suggest why they think the writer has chosen to make all the diary entries from July 31st to September 7th so short. How does it link with the atmosphere and Laura's state of mind? (The storm devastation and the Perryman family's loss of heart following Billy's departure.)

READ & RESPOND: Activities based on The Wreck of the Zanzibar

Guided reading

SECTION 2

September 8th – September 9th

These two diary entries give a vivid account of Laura's discovery of the turtle and her successful attempt to save it from death.

Read the section in the diary entry for September 8th; 'He was upside down on the sand… His flippers were quite still, and held out to the clouds above as if he was worshipping them.' Ask the children how they think this might link in Laura's mind to her own situation. (The turtle's position reminds Laura of praying, an act of hope. He is imprisoned, just as she and her family are trapped.)

Laura's actions to save the turtle show a mixture of her practical nature and generosity of spirit. Ask the class to look for examples of these actions, for example, pulling seaweed from the turtle, rocking it, levering it up (practical); making 'a pillow of soft sea lettuce' (generous).

At the end of the diary entry for September 8th, after her father has questioned her, Laura says: 'I should tell him. I know I should. But I can't do it. I just can't let them eat him.' The islanders are hungry. She has saved the turtle and hidden it. Do the children think her actions were selfish, or can they justify Laura's motivation for saving the turtle?

In the diary entry for September 9th, Laura opens her heart to the turtle. Ask the children why they think she does this. (Non-judgmental audience, unable to answer back.) Laura identifies the turtle's plight with her own. The turtle is imprisoned on the island and at the mercy of the elements, just as she and her family are. Encourage the children to identify clues which tell them about Laura's feelings, and why she tells the turtle everything that has happened so far. ('He's got eyes that make you think he understands.') Explain that, on another level, the episode gives the author a chance to recap the main events of the story so far.

Read the section when Granny May arrives on the beach. Ask the children to look for references in the text which infer how she feels about Laura's actions. (She doesn't question Laura about the morality of what she is doing but says 'Let's try shrimps.' This signals that she will help Laura to save the turtle.) As the children read on, ask them to find evidence for Granny May's and Laura's feelings as the turtle gets back into the sea. ('I went loony… The two of us whistled and whooped.')

Look at the section 'I felt suddenly alone… kissed the top of my head.' What can the children infer from this? (Laura feels lonely because the turtle leaving reminds her of Billy leaving.) Can the children find any indication of this near the end of the entry. ('If Billy were here I'd tell him.')

October 25th – December 8th

These diary entries are brief and depressing. All hope seems lost for Laura and her family and this is reflected in the darkness of the season.

Ask the class to search for words and phrases that contribute to the atmosphere of hopelessness. Encourage them to link phrases that describe the family's state of mind to those that describe what is actually happening on the island – the hunger, the cold wind, the storms and rain. (Examples of such phrases include: 'When no one talks it means we're all thinking of Billy…'; 'Mother looks so grey these days…'; The house creaks in the wind…'; 'crushed and sunken'.) Has the writer made these connections deliberately?

Ask the children which characters are lacking in hope, and to find evidence in the text to support their views. Who is the one person who keeps faith with the island? (Granny May.) What does she think the storms are telling them? (They are an omen telling the family to stay on Bryher.)

December 9th

The author describes the scene of the wreck with stunning imagery. Ask the children to skim through to collect words and phrases that describe the storm, for example, 'The sea surged and churned'; 'A witches' brew of wind and tide'. How does the author lend urgency to the situation? (Verbs such as 'staggered', 'hauled',

Guided reading

SECTION 2

'cursing', 'groaning'; the way the gig Chief speaks to his crew; the way the gig crew behave.)

Ask which two dreams are fulfilled. (Laura rows in the gig and Billy comes home.) The language is as turbulent as the sea until Laura sees Billy. Then calm is restored, and the sea is no longer against them ('the wind and the waves behind us…the gig flew over the sea'). Granny May does not seem surprised to see Billy. Ask why she whispers, 'The turtle, the turtle'. (Granny May believes that nature will reward one act of goodness with another. She and Laura returned the turtle to the sea and now Billy has been returned to them.) Discuss this point of view. Does Laura believe it? Do the children think it is true, or is Granny May a 'mad old stick' as most of the islanders think?

December 10th ~ 'Marzipan'

Although Billy is home there are other issues to resolve before Laura closes her diary. Ask the children what these are. (The loss of the cows, the damaged buildings.) The wreck of the *Zanzibar* brings an unexpected harvest for the islanders, and for the Perrymans in particular. What do Laura and the family salvage from the wreck that restores hope and provides a means for them to stay on the island? (The cows.) When the *Zanzibar* sinks everyone watches and some fall to their knees. Only one person remains standing. Ask the children who this is. (Granny May.) Why does she not kneel with the rest? (Old age, non-religious beliefs.)

The family are reconciled. Ask the class how both Billy's and Laura's views have changed throughout the story. (Billy believes there's nowhere like home. Laura has hope again.)

On Christmas Day the family receive a surprise present and Laura writes, 'It seems Granny May might have been right after all'. What is it that Granny May might have been right about, and what was washed up on the shore to make Laura think this? (The wooden turtle.) Granny May says, 'Now do you believe me?' What is she asking Laura to believe? (The link between the rescue of the turtle and the homecoming of Billy on a ship with a wooden turtle as a figurehead.)

In the last section, 'Marzipan', ask the children how they know that the narration has returned to the present. (Italics are not used.) Who takes over the story? (Michael.)

The author ingeniously links the events of the past with the present. How does he do this? (The family fulfilling Laura's last request and putting Zanzibar on the green for all the children of Bryher.) Discuss how the author pulls the threads of the story together and makes it live on in the present. (Through Michael retelling it to the rest of Great-aunt Laura's family.)

Shared reading

SECTION 3

Extract 1

- Display an enlarged photocopy of Extract 1. Read the extract to the class.
- Ask the children to identify the narrator (Laura) and the other main character in this extract (Billy).
- Read the extract again and ask them what they know about Laura – her age, where she lives, what she does and if she has any brothers or sisters.
- Ask them what her hopes and dreams are, as she begins her diary.
- Draw an outline of Laura on the board. Ask the children to suggest words and phrases from the extract which give information about Laura as a person. Write these inside the drawing of her outline.
- Now ask the children to tell you what they know about events, other people, places and actions in the story. Write these round the outside of the drawing.
- Discuss with the children how the writer has cleverly sewn all this information together without writing a list. Mention how the mirror reflects both Laura's own image, and her fantasy image (Lady Eugenia). Explain how she brings her brother Billy into her monologue through identifying her own hopes with his job as a member of the gig crew.

Extract 2

- Display an enlarged copy of Extract 2. Read the extract to the children.
- Ask the children to sequence the main events in the extract – Joseph Hannibal leaves, Billy and Laura have a row, Father and Billy have a row.
- Ask the children if they notice anything about the tense of the extract. (It changes from present to past.) Discuss the reasons for this. (A convention of the genre of diary writing – present thoughts followed by reflection.)
- Ask the children how the writer uses language to help build up the tension. (Short, simple sentences and verbs such as 'shrugged', 'grabbed', 'roared'.)
- Highlight the expressions 'split us apart', 'nose to nose' and 'eyes like steel'. Ask the class why the writer uses phrases like this. (Strong imagery to generate atmosphere.) What response does he hope to get from the reader? (To build tension and encourage feelings of empathy.)

Extract 3

- Display an enlarged copy of the extract and read it to the children. Ask them to imagine that they are Michael Morpurgo reading a draft of this extract, checking that the language used will evoke the images he wants the reader to picture.
- Re-read the text. Suggest words and phrases that have been used to create the scene. Circle these or write them on the board, for example, 'We hung over our oars'; 'tumbled over the side'; 'the gig groaned and cried'; 'A thunderous wave reared up'.
- Look for the use of alliteration, for example, 'a great green wall of water'; 'witches' brew of wind'. How does this enhance the text? Do the children think these phrases are effective?
- Ask the children to make alternative suggestions for the words and phrases collected. Do they think Michael Morpurgo might have thought of these too? If he did, why do they think he rejected them?
- Discuss the way in which the Chief speaks to the crew. Are these orders? Are they spoken or shouted? Ask the children to imagine that they are the Chief 'lifting' with the crew, 'bellowing' at them and 'clearing the way ahead.' Why does he do this? (To urge the crew on.)

READ & RESPOND: Activities based on The Wreck of the Zanzibar

Shared reading

Extract 1

January 20th

"Laura Perryman, you are fourteen years old today."

I said that to the mirror this morning when I wished myself "Happy Birthday". Sometimes, like this morning, I don't much want to be Laura Perryman, who's lived on Bryher all her life and milks cows. I want to be Lady Eugenia Fitzherbert with long red hair and green eyes, who wears a big wide hat with a white ostrich feather and who travels the world in steamships with four funnels. But then, I also want to be Billy Perryman so I can row out in the gig and build boats and run fast. Billy's fourteen too – being my twin brother, he would be. But I'm not Lady Eugenia Fitzherbert, whoever she is, and I'm not Billy; I'm me. I'm Laura Perryman and I'm fourteen years old today.

Everyone is pleased with me, even Father, because I was the one who spotted the ship before they did on St Mary's. It was just that I was in the right place at the right time, that's all. I'd been milking the cows with Billy, as usual, and I was coming back with the buckets over Watch Hill when I saw sails on the horizon out beyond White Island. It looked like a schooner, three-masted. We left the buckets and ran all the way home.

The gig was launched in five minutes. I watched the whole thing from the top of Samson Hill with everyone else. We saw the St Mary's gig clear the harbour wall, the wind and the tide in her favour. The race was on. For some time it looked as if the St Mary's gig would reach the schooner first, as she so often does, but we found clear water and a fair wind out beyond Samson and we were flying along.

Shared reading

Extract 2

February 15th

This is the worst day of my whole life. It began well. Joseph Hannibal left the house this morning at last. I thought he'd sail away on the evening tide and that would be the end of him. I was wrong. Billy has gone with him. Even as I write it, I can hardly believe it. Billy has gone.

It all began just after Joseph Hannibal left. We've had arguments before, Billy and me, but never like this. He didn't seem a bit sad when I told him, at last, about Molly and her calf. He just said that I should have been there, or Mother; that it wasn't his fault. I got angry and shouted at him. Billy just shrugged and walked off. I hate it when he does that. I raced after him and grabbed him. He turned on me and told me I was taking Father's side against him. I knew then that it was all because of Joseph Hannibal. It's as if he's split us apart. Billy thinks that everything about him is wonderful, that he's doing what a proper man should. He won't hear a word against him.

This afternoon Billy and Father had their expected set-to about Molly. Father roared and of course Billy shouted back at him. He wasn't going to stay and be a cowman all his life, he had better things to be doing. I've never seen Billy like it. The angrier he became, the more he seemed to grow. Nose to nose in the kitchen he was as big as Father. Father said he'd strap him if he didn't hold his tongue and Billy just stared at him and said nothing, his eyes like steel.

Shared reading

Extract 3

December 9th

We hung over our oars like wet rags, drained of all strength. But the Chief hadn't finished with us yet.

"Out!" he cried, and he leapt over the side. "We'll carry her across Samson and launch her again on the other side. It's the only way we'll reach them. Come on, you beggars. Be time to rest when it's done."

So we tumbled over the side, lashed the oars again and lifted. The neck of Samson is just a hundred yards or so across, but in the teeth of that gale, it felt like a mile. More than once I stumbled and fell to my knees, but always there were strong hands grasping me and hauling me to my feet.

"I can see them!" cried the Chief. "Over on White Island. I can see them."

The Chief was everywhere, lifting with us, bellowing behind us, clearing the way ahead of us. We reached the beach on the far side of Samson at last and ran the gig down over the pebbles until the sea took the weight of her from us. We unlashed the oars, pushed her out and piled in.

"Pull!" he cried. "Pull for your children, pull for your wives."

I have no children, I have no wife, but I pulled all the same. I pulled instead for Granny May, for Mother, for Father and for Billy, especially for Billy.

It was no great distance across the narrow channel but the seas were seething. A witches' brew of wind and tide and current took us and tossed us about at will. Under us the gig groaned and cried, but she held together. A thunderous wave reared up above us, a great green wall of water and I thought we must go over.

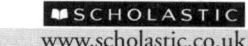

Plot, character and setting

SECTION 4

A sense of place

Objectives: To consider how texts can be rooted in the writer's experience; to describe a situation from another point of view.
What you need: Photocopiable page 15; a map of the Scilly Isles, copies of the book.
Cross-curricular links: Art and design, Unit 6C, A sense of place; Geography, Unit 23, Investigating coasts.

What to do
- Explain that *The Wreck of the Zanzibar* is set in a real place – the Isles of Scilly. Look at the map of the islands and discuss any place names that children may recognise.
- Talk about writers using their own experience as the basis for their books. Michael Morpurgo has used a real setting and a real period of history in *The Wreck of the Zanzibar*, although the events and characters are fictional.
- Read the first diary entry (January 20th), from 'Laura Perryman, you are fourteen years old...' to '...ran all the way home.' On the whiteboard, make a note of the place names that are mentioned. (Bryher, St Mary's, Watch Hill, White Island.) Point out that Laura doesn't explain these places. This gives the story authenticity – it is a young girl's personal account of her own world.
- Talk about the book's setting. Laura and Billy know their island and its community intimately. Talk about the advantages and disadvantages of this. Can the children find evidence that Laura and Billy dream of adventure in a wider world? ('travels the world in steamships'; 'an American ship... bound for New York.')
- Discuss how Michael Morpurgo has created a world that is both strange and familiar, and that is totally believable.
- Hand out copies of the photocopiable sheet and ask children to complete it.

Differentiation
For older/more able children: Encourage the children to compare the events in their account of their approach to Bryher with the account in the book. They could also add extra names of places and features, based on a modern-day map.
For younger/less able children: Read the entry carefully with the children and discuss what Bryher looks like. Ask the children to draw a picture of one of the scenes described, based on the text (for example, the Bryher people watching from the top of the hill).

School reports

Objective: To investigate how characters are presented.
What you need: Photocopiable page 16, writing materials, copies of the book.

What to do
- Discuss the different ways that characters are presented in this story – through what they say, what they do, or how they are described. Look at how Laura and Billy relate to each other and the other characters in the book. Explore the children's own responses to the characters. (Is Billy brave or childish when he runs away?)
- Hand out the photocopiable sheet. Ask half the class to imagine that they are Laura's teacher and the other half to imagine they are Billy's teacher. Ask the groups to write end-of-year reports for Billy and Laura. They should use the text to find out about: Laura's and Billy's interests; their favourite subjects at school; their good qualities; things they might need to improve on!

Differentiation
For older/more able children: Ask the children to list Laura's best qualities and her worst. They should look for clues in the diary and discuss their findings.
For younger/less able children: Ask them to find diary entries that reveal Laura's character, then draw a picture of Laura and write their findings around it.

Plot, character and setting

SECTION 4

What's the plot?

Objective: To identify the key features of a literary text, for example, plot structure.
What you need: Writing materials, a flipchart or board, copies of the book.

What to do
- Explain that *The Wreck of the Zanzibar* uses a common plot structure:
1) Complication (the event that starts the story).
2) Tension builders (dramatic events that follow).
3) Climax (the most dramatic event of all).
4) Resolution (the point where dramatic events and tensions are resolved).
- Explore the diary section of the book with the children. Divide them into three groups. Each group should look for one of the following:
  - The complication within Laura's diary. (The arrival of Joseph Hannibal, Billy's departure.)
  - The tension-builders that occur up until the shipwreck. (Worsening weather, damage to buildings, the cows dying.)
  - The climax and the resolution in the diary. (The wreck, the rescue and finding Billy.)
- Discuss the children's findings, writing notes on the flipchart.

Differentiation
For older/more able children: Ask the children to look at the beginning and the end of the book (the sections in italics), and identify the complication, the tension builders, the climax and the resolution.
For younger/less able children: Help the children to understand the difference between the climax and the resolution of the story. Discuss how the climax is the most exciting event in the story. Show them how it leads to the resolution. (Billy's return puts everything right again – but this would not have happened had the ship not been wrecked.)

Word pictures

Objectives: To understand the differences between literal and figurative language, for example, through discussing the effects of imagery in prose; to describe and evaluate the style of an individual writer.
What you need: Writing materials, copies of the book.

What to do
- Explain to the children that writers often use words to paint pictures in their readers' minds.
- Explain that the quality of the words chosen, and how they are put together, creates the writer's unique style.
- Read the diary entry for December 9th, from 'The rain was coming in hail squalls…' to '…where we were dumped high and safe on the shingle of White Island.'
- In small groups, ask the children to collect words and phrases that describe:
  - The violence of the storm.
  - The actions of the gig crew.
- Encourage them to think about the writer's careful use of words to describe the gig crew's actions. Make a list of verbs and adverbs on the flipchart. Can they tell from the use of verbs and adverbs if the task is easy or hard? Then make a list of nouns and adjectives. What picture is the writer creating in the reader's mind? How does he build tension and excitement?
- Talk about the effect of well-chosen adverbs, adjectives or verbs in creating a vivid image.

Differentiation
For older/more able children: They should write down words and phrases from the entry for November 30th that describe the atmosphere in the Perryman household and the weather's effect on the islanders. Discuss which they like best, and why.
For younger/less able children: Using the diary entry for September 6th, ask the children to collect words or phrases that describe the storm. Ask them to talk about the words and phrases they like best.

READ & RESPOND: Activities based on *The Wreck of the Zanzibar*

Plot, character and setting

SECTION 4

Reading between the lines

Objective: To develop an active attitude towards reading.
What you need: Writing materials, copies of the book.
Cross-curricular links: Science, Unit 6A, Interdependence and adaptation.

What to do
- Explain to the class that sometimes the characters or narrator tell us what is happening, and sometimes we have to look for clues through what they say, how they react and what they do. This is called 'inference'.
- Read the diary entry for September 8th from, 'I looked around, and there were more gulls gathering' to '…his eyes closed to the world.' Ask the children to find verbs that describe Laura's actions. What can they infer from these words? Is her task difficult? How does she cope? What does this tell them about Laura's character?
- Read the diary entry for September 9th, from 'I felt suddenly alone.' to 'My wrist aches.' Ask the children to find words or phrases that tell them:
  - How Laura feels when the turtle has gone. ('I felt suddenly alone'.)
  - How Granny May feels towards Laura. ('…kissed the top of my head.')
  - About Laura's relationship with her Mother. ('I can't talk to her like I used to.')
  - That this has been a long diary entry. ('My wrist aches.')

Differentiation
For older/more able children: Ask the children to read the diary extract for December 25th. Tell them to find phrases inferring that Laura begins to think Granny May 'might have been right after all'.
For younger/less able children: Read the diary extract for December 6th. Help the children find words or phrases that tell us how Granny May feels about the situation and why she wants to stay.

The passage of time

Objective: To understand aspects of narrative structure – how authors handle time, for example, stories within stories; how the passing of time is conveyed to the reader.
What you need: Photocopiable page 17.

What to do
- Discuss the 'story within a story' structure of the book. How is the enclosing story different to the diary? (It is in italic; it isn't in diary format; it has a different narrator.) No dates are given, but it is obvious that it takes place in the present. What evidence can the children find for this?
- Discuss how the passage of time is conveyed in the diary – each entry has a date. Discuss how the main events happen in 'clusters' of entries:
  - January and February entries describe the arrival of the *General Lee* and Billy leaving.
  - Three diary entries describe how the family is affected by Billy's departure.
  - Four consecutive diary entries in September describe the storm and the turtle's rescue.
  - November and December's entries describe the storm, the wreck, and Billy's return.
- Ask the children why they think there are long gaps between some entries. Does it make the diary feel more 'real'? Great-aunt Laura says in her letter, 'I didn't write in it very often, just whenever I felt like it.'
- Ask the children to complete the photocopiable sheet.

Differentiation
For older/more able children: Ask them to look at the extract for September 6th and explore how the author uses different tenses to move back and forth in time.
For younger/less able children: Read the diary entry for February 14th with the children. Write three headings on a large piece of paper: Morning; Afternoon; Evening. Encourage the children to list the events of the day in order.

Plot, character and setting

SECTION 4

Beginnings, middles and ends

> **Objective:** To analyse the features of a good opening; to understand aspects of narrative structure, for example, how chapters in a book are linked together.
> **What you need:** Photocopiable page 18, flipchart or board, copies of the book.

What to do
- Read the opening chapter, 'Great-aunt Laura', and ask the children to suggest events that bring the characters into the story. (The funeral; the gift of the diary.) Write their ideas on the flipchart.
- Discuss the questions raised in this chapter. What makes them want to read on? (The gift of the diary; the mystery of 'Zanzibar'.)
- Read the final chapter. How are the readers' questions resolved? (Michael knows where Zanzibar came from, he passes on the story, and moves Zanzibar to where Laura wanted him.)
- Discuss the importance of the turtle. At the opening of the final chapter there is a picture of a child sitting on Zanzibar, and Michael sits on him to tell the children Laura's story. The turtle is a link between different times and generations of the family; between the family and the outside world; between the land and the sea; between the beginning of the story and the end.
- Ask children to fill in photocopiable page 18.

> **Differentiation**
> **For older/more able children:** Encourage the children to find the links between Laura's actions to save the turtle and Catherine's actions towards Zanzibar. (Tries to feed him, instigates moving him.)
> **For younger/less able children:** Draw attention to the phrase 'He only eats jellyfish' in the final chapter. Show how this relates to the entry for September 9th, when Laura and Granny May try to feed the turtle.

The gathering storm

> **Objective:** To analyse the success of texts and writers in evoking particular responses in the reader.
> **What you need:** Writing materials, copies of the book.

What to do
- Read the diary extracts from July 21st to September 6th. Tell the children that Michael Morpurgo is creating a response in the reader by linking events in the natural world to what is happening within Laura's family.
- Split the class into two groups. Ask one group to read diary extracts for July 21st and 30th. They should:
    - Identify the settings in the entries and make simple labelled sketches. (Billy's room, the barn, the church, Laura's room at night.)
    - Collect phrases from the text that describe Laura's state of mind and write them down on the sketches. ('That's when I miss Billy most'; 'You only get disappointed if you hope.')
- Ask the other group to read diary entries July 31st and August 23rd. They should:
    - Identify and sketch the settings. (The barn, the top of Samson Hill.)
    - Collect words and phrases that describe Laura's views on hope and write them down on the sketches.
- Bring the class together to share their findings. Discuss how Michael Morpurgo builds up a picture of the way Laura's family have become 'strangers to each other' since Billy has left.

> **Differentiation**
> **For older/more able children:** Encourage more able children to explore the themes of 'hope' and 'hopelessness', and how this is reflected in the natural world, in other parts of the book.
> **For younger/less able children:** Make the connection between the weather and the family's situation more explicit for the children. Choose one setting and examine in detail the feelings of Laura and other characters within it.

READ & RESPOND: Activities based on The Wreck of the Zanzibar

Plot, character and setting

SECTION 4

A sense of place

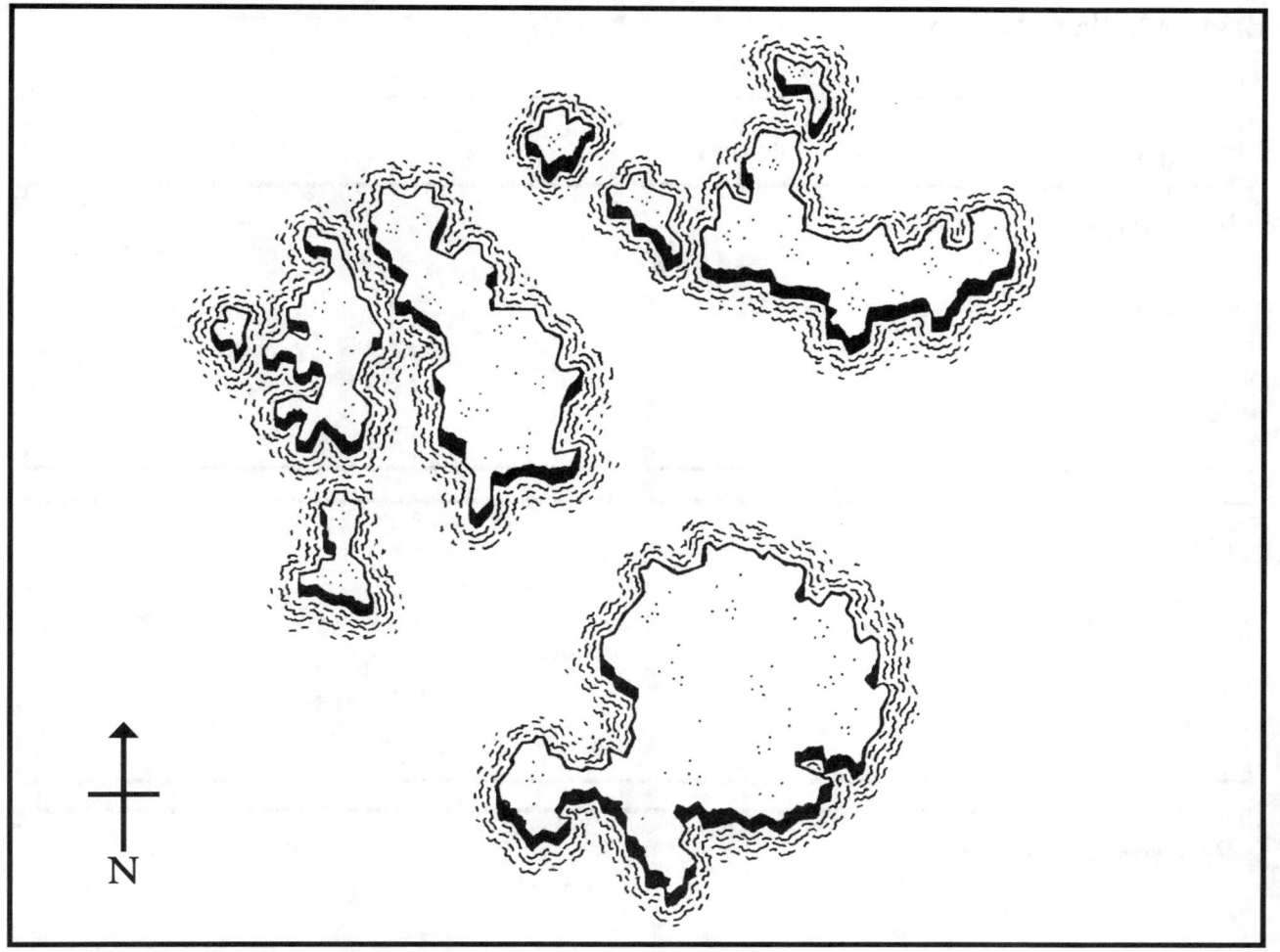

Illustration © The Drawing Room

1) Add place names to the map. Use the book to help you.
2) Show the routes that the Bryher gig and the *General Lee* took on January 20th.
3) Imagine you were one of the crew on the *General Lee* that day. Describe your approach to the Isles of Scilly:

PHOTOCOPIABLE

SCHOLASTIC
www.scholastic.co.uk

PAGE 15

READ & RESPOND: Activities based on The Wreck of the Zanzibar

Plot, character and setting

SECTION 4

School reports

Bryher Village School

Name: _____

Date: July 1906   Age: 14 years

Favourite subjects

Interests

Personal qualities

Things to improve

Signed: _____   (Class teacher)

PHOTOCOPIABLE

READ & RESPOND: Activities based on The Wreck of the Zanzibar

SCHOLASTIC
www.scholastic.co.uk

Plot, character and setting

SECTION 4

The passage of time

1) The diary section in *The Wreck of the Zanzibar* takes place over a year. Mark the diary entries on to the timeline. Make brief notes in the boxes about what happens for each cluster of events.

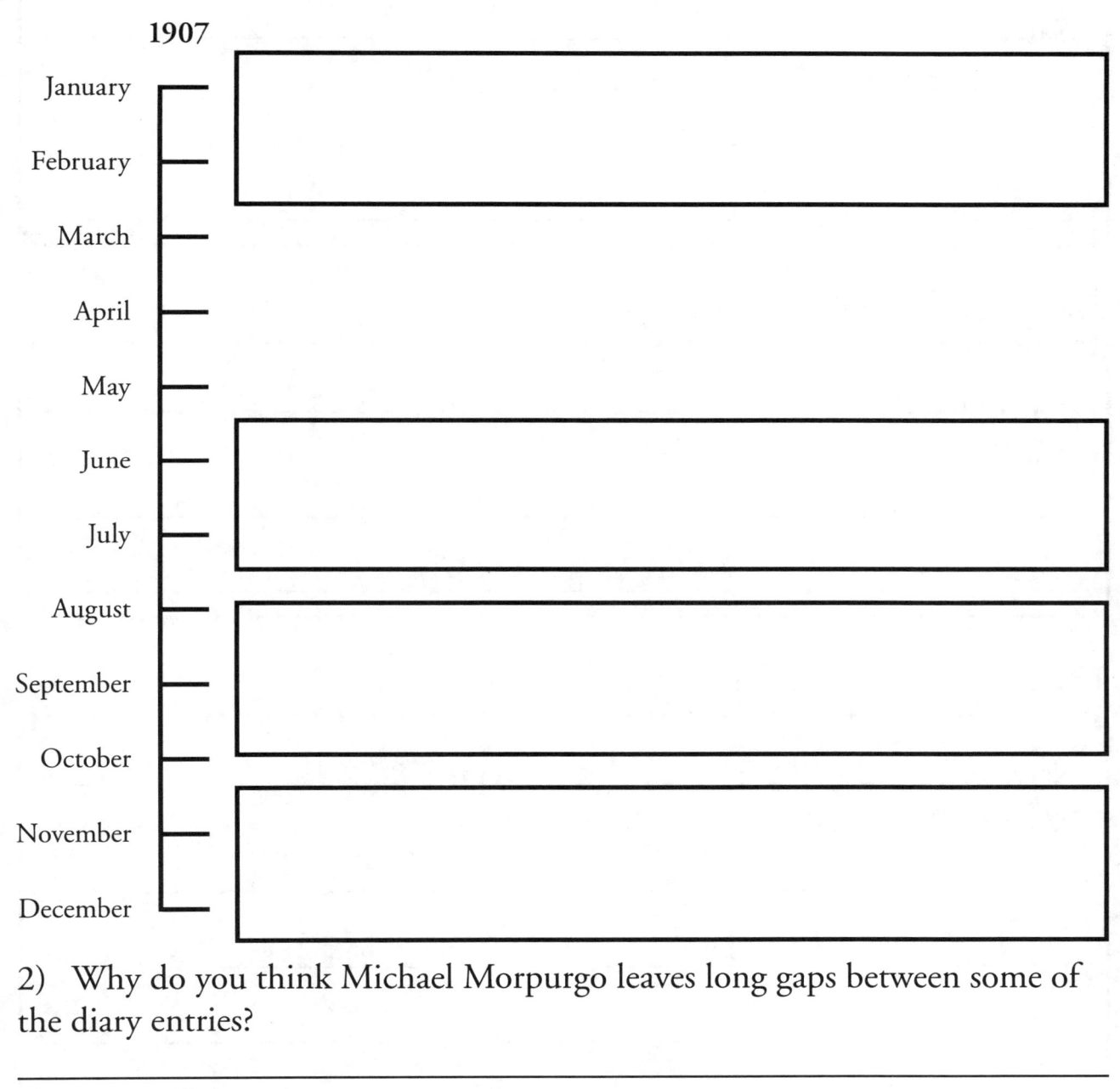

1907

January
February
March
April
May
June
July
August
September
October
November
December

2) Why do you think Michael Morpurgo leaves long gaps between some of the diary entries?

___

PHOTOCOPIABLE

Plot, character and setting

SECTION 4

Beginnings, middles and ends

1) Complete the chart below.
The opening: 'Great-aunt Laura'

```
Narrator: _____ Time: _____
What makes the reader want to find out more?
_____
_____
```

The middle: 'The Diary of Laura Perryman'

```
Narrator: _____ Time: _____
What does the reader find out?
_____
_____
```

The conclusion: 'Marzipan'

```
Narrator: _____ Time: _____
What make this a satisfying ending for the reader?
_____
_____
_____
_____
```

Talk about it

SECTION 5

Funeral guests

Objective: To analyse and evaluate how speakers present points effectively, through use of language and gesture.
What you need: Copies of the book, flipchart or whiteboard.
Cross-curricular links: Drama.

What to do
- Read the opening chapter, 'Great-aunt Laura'. Discuss who the other people at the funeral are. (Friends and relatives of Great-aunt Laura.) Ask the children to suggest names for them, and their relationship to Laura. Write these on the flipchart or board.
- Tell the children that you want them to create a character around one of these names, and role play it.
- Arrange the children into groups of five and ask each member of the group to choose a different character from the list on the board. Each child should think about their character's memories of Great-aunt Laura, deciding whether these are good or bad. They should also consider how they will use language and gesture to build their character.
- The groups should discuss the conversation that its different members will have. Allow ten minutes for them to rehearse what their characters will say.
- Ask the children to create a still image of their group (a freeze-frame). Tell them you are going to be Uncle Will. You will go to each group in turn. As you come to each group, they should unfreeze and begin their conversation. At the end of their conversation, they go back into a freeze-frame and you move on to the next group. Remind them that they must be still and silent while the other groups are talking.
- To finish, discuss what they liked about each other's characterisations. How did they make them effective?

Differentiation
For older/more able children: Michael is in his old bedroom in the cottage. He phones home and talks to his wife. What do they say to each other? Ask the children to create this conversation in pairs.
For younger/less able children: Ask the children to work in pairs, imagining that they are a parent and child attending the funeral. Ask them to create a conversation about who, or what, 'Zanzibar' is.

Story-telling

Objective: To tell a story using notes; to use techniques, such as repetition, recap and humour.
What you need: Copies of the books, art materials.
Cross-curricular links: Drama and art.

What to do
- Tell the children that they are going to retell Laura's story to each other. Group the children in pairs and give each pair a section of the story.
- Ask the pairs to read their section and make notes. They will use the notes to make cue cards, to help them retell the story. They should first plot the main sequence of events. They can then add further details, to help them tell the story.
- Encourage the children who are not speaking to prepare sound effects and images to enhance the story-telling. These could include sounds of the sea, the gulls and the storm, or a picture of the sea for a backdrop.
- Ask each pair to retell their diary entry to a different pair. Then ask the pairs in turn to tell their section of the story to the rest of the class.

Differentiation
For older/more able children: Ask the children to retell the longest sections in the diary – the turtle episode, and the day the *Zanzibar* is wrecked.
For younger/less able children: Ask the children to retell the shortest sections, such as the introduction.

Talk about it

SECTION 5

The argument

Objective: To improvise, using a range of drama strategies and conventions, to explore themes such as hopes and fears. For example, drawing on shared text to explore emotional tension at key moments in a story.
What you need: Copies of the book, flipchart.

What to do
- Read the part of the entry for February 15th where Billy and his Father have their argument.
- Write the names of the characters in this scene on the flipchart or board. (Billy, Father, Laura, Mother.)
- Talk about how the dialogue between Billy and Father is reported by Laura. We are not given the actual words. Nor are we told what is going through Mother and Laura's minds.
- Choose two children to role play Billy and Father. Ask them to work out a brief dialogue for the scene, using the text as a starting point.
- Divide the rest of the children into two groups. Ask one group to imagine Laura's emotions as she watches the argument, and the other group to do the same for Mother.
- When each group is ready, ask them to sit in the circle. The children representing Billy and Father should stand in the middle, nose to nose, and speak their dialogue. At appropriate points, stop the action and ask a member from each of the two groups to speak the thoughts of Mother and Laura.

Differentiation
For older/more able children: Read the text from November 30th to December 8th. Ask the children to create a monologue for Granny May, showing her view of things, for one of the group to perform.
For younger/less able children: Ask the children to read the diary entry for October 25th and create a dialogue between Laura and Father as they paint the gig. Think about her request (to row in the gig) and how he reacts.

The birthday party

Objective: To devise a performance considering how it should be adapted for a specific audience.
What you need: Copies of the book, photocopiable page 22.
Cross-curricular links: Drama.

What to do
- Read the description of the birthday party held for Laura and Billy in the diary entry for January 20th.
- Tell the children they are going to devise a short scene based on this text, to perform to younger children. They must keep their language and dialogue in keeping with the story but also at a level that can be understood by the intended audience.
- Divide the class into groups. The children should decide which of the following characters they want to be: Laura, Billy, Mother, Father, Granny May, the Chief of the gig crew and the four other members of the gig crew.
- Each child should first fill in the photocopiable sheet, for their character.
- The groups should then work out a script for the scene. They should think carefully about how the atmosphere and characters' feelings change when Laura makes her request.
- Before they start rehearsing their scripts, remind the children of their audience. Encourage them to check through the script, making sure that it will appeal to, and be understood by, younger children.

Differentiation
For older/less able children: Ensure these children take the bigger parts in the script.
For younger/less able children: Ensure these children take the smaller parts in the script.

Talk about it

SECTION 5

The island debate

Objective: To participate in a whole-class debate using the conventions and language of debate, including standard English.
What you need: Photocopiable page 23.

What to do
- Tell the children to imagine that Laura and Granny May have been seen rescuing the turtle. The island Chief calls a meeting at which the two must account for their actions.
- Explain to the class that they are going to take part in a debate. The motion is 'Were Granny May and Laura right to rescue the turtle?'
- Divide the class into two groups. One group will argue for Granny May and Laura, and the other group will argue against. Each child must choose a role for the debate. The main speakers for the side against Granny May and Laura will be the Chief and Father. The main speakers for the opposing side will be Granny May, Laura and Mother.
- The defending group must use the text to justify the actions of Laura and Granny May.
- The attacking group must use the text to condemn the actions of Laura and Granny May.
- Each group should make notes to back up their argument on the photocopiable sheet, and list some questions to ask the other group.
- Hold the debate, and take a vote at the end.

Differentiation
For older/more able children: Ask these children to take on the roles of Laura and Granny May, and Father and the Chief. Ask them to present their case to the rest of the islanders.
For younger/less able children: Help the children to frame good questions to put to the main speakers.

News report!

Objective: To consider the overall impact of a live or recorded performance, identifying dramatic ways of conveying characters' ideas and building tension.
What you need: Photocopiable page 24, a video camera (optional).
Cross-curricular links: Citizenship, Unit 11, In the media – what's the news?

What to do
- Show a video of a television news report to the children. Discuss the format of the report with them.
- Ask the children to read the diary entry for December 9th.
- Hand out copies of the photocopiable sheet. Ask the children to make a storyboard of six key events from the diary entry to include in a news report. (For example, a shot of the sea, the ship foundering, or the gig setting out and so on.) They should then write down a list of key questions to ask in interviews for a report.
- Arrange the children into pairs to conduct an interview. One of the pair should role play the presenter and the other should role play a character involved in the rescue. They should base the interview on the notes they have made.
- Ask the children to present their interviews to the rest of the class as a news report for December 9th, 1907.
- If you have a video camera in school, film the interviews and show them as part of a school assembly. Alternatively, record the interviews on to an audio cassette.

Differentiation
For older/more able children: Ask the children to make up a commentary to accompany the film of the *Zanzibar* foundering, and the gig going to the rescue.
For younger/less able children: Work with this group to write an introduction for the presenter of the news report. They should mention the setting, the date, the time, which television company they represent, and a summary of what happened.

Talk about it

SECTION 5

The birthday party

My character is:

What happens…	How my character might feel:	What my character might say:
Granny May comes in with the birthday cake.		
Everybody eats the birthday cake.		
Everybody sings Happy Birthday to Laura and Billy.		
The Chief of the gig makes a speech.		
Laura makes her request.		
Everybody reacts to the request.		
Laura leaves the party.		

PHOTOCOPIABLE

READ & RESPOND: Activities based on The Wreck of the Zanzibar

www.scholastic.co.uk

Talk about it

SECTION 5

The island debate

The motion is: **Were Granny May and Laura right to rescue the turtle?**
Is your group for or against?

What reasons will you put forward to support your position?

What questions would you like to ask the other group?

Talk about it

SECTION 5

News report!

1) Read the diary entry for December 9th.
2) Make a storyboard showing six key events from the entry, to include in a news report.

3) Make a list of key people to interview:

_____

_____

4) Write down some questions that you could ask in the interview:

_____

_____

_____

_____

_____

_____

Get writing

SECTION 6

Dear diary...

Objectives: To write in the style of the author, for example, writing a new chapter; to write from another character's point of view, for example, retelling an incident in letter form.
What you need: Copies of the book, writing materials.

What to do
- Divide the class into two groups.
- Ask one group to imagine that they are Michael. Tell them he has returned home, with the diary, after the funeral. He sits in his bedroom and decides that he will keep his own diary. Ask the children to write his first diary entry. (Is it about his memories of Great-aunt Laura? Is it full of regrets because he has not been to the island for some time? How come he has not been across to Bryher for a while?)
- Ask the second group to imagine that they are Michael standing in his old bedroom in Great-aunt Laura's cottage. He remembers being eight years old again and the holidays he spent there. Ask the children to write a diary entry, telling of the fondest memory from his childhood holidays.
- Choose children from both groups to share their diary entries with the class.

Differentiation
For older/more able children: Ask this group to imagine they are Uncle Will. Write a letter from him to his wife, describing the funeral. What does he think of Michael, and of Laura's diary?
For younger/less able children: Ask this group to imagine they are Michael at the age of eight. Write a postcard from him to Great-aunt Laura thanking her for a wonderful holiday. Help them include Michael's happiest holiday memory as part of the postcard.

Gig racing

Objective: To write non-chronological reports linked to other subjects.
What you need: Internet access, library access, writing materials.
Cross-curricular links: PE, Unit 30, Outdoor and adventurous activities; ICT, Unit 6D, Using the internet.

What to do
- Tell the children that they are going to write a report about gig racing. Explain that this is a traditional and popular sport in Cornwall and the Isles of Scilly, and remind them that rowing in the gig was Laura's burning ambition.
- Talk to the children about the requirements of writing non-chronological reports: an introduction to orientate reader, the use of the present tense, and impersonal language.
- Tell the children that they will be working in threes. They will use their ICT skills to research information about gig boats, which will help them prepare their report.
- Supervise the children in some internet research, to find out as much as they can about gigs and gig racing. Give them suggestions about areas to research. These might include:
  - The history of gig boat racing – how it all started and what happens now.
  - The way gigs are made – they could collect information in note form, and draw a labelled plan of a gig.
  - Famous tales about gig boats – they may come across a rescue made by a gig from Bryher, which links to Laura's diary!
- The children should use the information they have collected to write their report.

Differentiation
For older/more able children: The children should research all the above aspects about gigs and include labelled pictures and diagrams.
For younger/less able children: Simplify the activity by restricting the number of headings (for example, looking only at modern-day gig racing).

READ & RESPOND: Activities based on The Wreck of the Zanzibar

Get writing

SECTION 6

Welcome to Bryher

Objective: To select an appropriate style and form to suit a specific purpose and audience, drawing on knowledge of different types of non-fiction texts.
What you need: Photocopiable page 28; examples of advertising brochures, access to the internet and library resources.
Cross-curricular links: ICT, Unit 6D, Using the internet; Geography, Unit 23, Investigating coasts.

What to do
- Ask the children to imagine they are Michael. He has decided to buy his Great-aunt Laura's cottage and run it as a bed and breakfast for holiday-makers. He decides to create an advertising brochure for the cottage, to attract people to Bryher and his cottage.
- Show the children examples of advertising brochures. Explain that they are going to use ICT and research skills to make their own brochure to advertise the cottage.
- Tell the children that they are going to work in pairs to make notes on the following using information from the book, and other information they find through their own research:
  - What makes the cottage an attractive place to stay? Include historical information on Laura and the wreck of the *Zanzibar*.
  - Interesting information about the Scilly Isles – nearby places to visit, things to see and do, information on how to get there.
- Ask them to collect their information on the photocopiable sheet.
- Invite the children to design their brochures, and share some of them with the class. Display them where everyone can see them.

Differentiation
For older/more able children: Encourage these children to carry out in-depth research. They could include maps and boat timetables.
For younger/less able children: Help them to structure their research for the leaflet, concentrating on the cottage and its location. It may be helpful to make a simpler template into which they can write.

Writing a playscript

Objective: To prepare a short section of story as a script, using the correct conventions, for instance, stage directions and setting.
What you need: Copies of the book, photocopiable page 29, writing materials.

What to do
- Read the diary entry for November 30th.
- Hand out the photocopiable sheet and read through the script. Point out that the scene is not actually in the book, but is based on clues from the text. (For example, limpets and potatoes for tea.)
- Talk about the conventions of a playscript. Discuss how the setting is indicated, and how stage directions tell the characters how to act. Talk about the way the character's name is set apart from the speech, and how italics are used.
- Ask when this conversation took place. (Just before Father's speech starting 'If he's going…')
- Divide the children into groups, and ask them to continue writing the scene. They should use the text to work out who says what, and add directions as to how the characters act. Encourage them to set the playscript out correctly.
- Each group should then prepare their scene. Bring the class together and ask each group to perform the scene for the rest of the class.

Differentiation
For older/more able children: Ask the children to work in pairs to prepare another scene, based on the entry for September 9th, from 'A sudden shadow fell across me' to '…kissed the top of my head.'
For younger/less able children: Look at the entry for September 8th. Help the children to identify the direct speech in the section from 'You all right?' to 'Just things.' Discuss how we know who is speaking. Help them turn the extract into a scripted dialogue.

Get writing

SECTION 6

Diary writing

> **Objective:** To use different genres as models for writing – for example, short extracts, sequels, additional episodes, alternative endings – using appropriate conventions and language.
> **What you need:** Photocopiable page 30, writing materials.

What to do
- Read the extracts on photocopiable page 30 to the children. Tell them that both are examples of fictional diaries. One is from the diary of a boy aged 13 ¾. The other is the diary of a girl who is also about the same age as Laura.
- Discuss the styles used. Which is humorous, and which is serious? Were they set recently or in the past? Discuss the use of language and the style of writing in both extracts. How do they differ, if at all, from Laura's diary? For example, they should notice Adrian's conversational style and his use of short sentences.
- Ask the children to work with a partner. For each extract, they should write entries for the day before and the day after. Each child in the pair should write two extracts, one for each diary.
- Next, ask the children to discuss their entries with their partner, to see if they agree with what the other has done, and if there is anything they think could be changed or improved. Ask some of the pairs to read their entries out, and discuss their effectiveness as a class.

> **Differentiation**
> **For older/more able children:** Extend the activity by asking the children to write an extract from Pandora's diary. What kind of person is she? What would her writing style be like? What might she say about not wanting to go out with Adrian anymore? And about Craig Thomas!
> **For younger/less able children:** Restrict the activity to one diary style. Structure the activity by discussing what might have happened the day before and the day after the given diary entry.

Writing a review

> **Objective:** To write a brief helpful review tailored for real audiences.
> **What you need:** Examples of reviews of children's books, flipchart or board.

What to do
- Explain to the children that they are going to write a review of *The Wreck of the Zanzibar* for a school magazine.
- Read some reviews of children's books to the class.
- Put three headings up on the flipchart or board: Synopsis; Structure and style; Reader appeal. Ask the children what they think a book review should include and write their ideas under the headings. (A short synopsis of the story outlining the plot, the characters and the setting; some comments on the narrative structure – the diary form and use of two voices to tell the story; the style of writing – use of language, creation of atmosphere; whether it appeals to boys and girls; whether it retains the reader's interest.)
- Ask the children to write a short review, either by hand or on a computer.
- Invite groups to share their reviews with the rest of the class. Discuss what the class liked about each review.
- Display the reviews in the classroom.

> **Differentiation**
> **For older/more able children:** Ask the children to create a back cover for the latest edition of the book. They should write a blurb, with illustrations, that will make people want to read it.
> **For younger/less able children:** Structure the review for the children, giving them headings to help them organise their information. (For example, 'Book details', 'Plot summary', 'What's good about the book', 'What's not good about the book'.)

Get writing

SECTION 6

Welcome to Bryher

Use this template to collect notes for your brochure about the holiday cottage on Bryher.

| Name and picture of the cottage: | How to get there: |

| About Laura and the wreck of the *Zanzibar*: |

| About Bryher: | Places to go, things to do: |

PHOTOCOPIABLE

READ & RESPOND: Activities based on The Wreck of the Zanzibar

Get writing

SECTION 6

Writing a playscript

In the following scene, Laura's father makes an important decision…

The Wreck of the Zanzibar

Act Two: Scene one

The kitchen in the Perryman's cottage. It is supper time. Granny May and Laura are sitting at the table. Father is standing looking out of the window. Mother is not in the kitchen as the scene opens. Laura is writing her diary and Granny May is peeling a few potatoes for tea.

Father: This weather! When will it ever stop?

Granny May: It's how it's always been here. You have to live with it, that's all there is to it.

Laura: You've got to have hope. Isn't that what you always say, Granny?

Mother enters with a bowl of limpets. Granny May smiles at Laura and pats her hand. Father turns from the window.

Father: Huh! Hope! The more you hope, the more hopeless it seems.

Mother: Something'll turn up.

Father walks over to the table.

Father: Not this time. It's over.

Mother: Over?

Continue the scene from here. Remember to read the whole diary extract before you begin. Look for clues about:
- What other people on the island are saying and doing.
- What Father means by 'It's over.'
- What Granny May might say about his decision.
- How Laura, Mother and Granny May might react to Father's decision.

Get writing

SECTION 6

Diary writing

1) Read these two diary extracts.

Diary extract 1
(From *The Secret Diary of Adrian Mole aged 13¾* by Sue Townsend)

Diary extract 2
(From *Blitz: The Diary of Edie Benson, London 1940–1941* by Vince Cross)

Tuesday April 7th

My precious Pandora is going out with Craig Thomas.

That's the last time you get a Mars bar from me, Thomas!

Barry Kent is in trouble for drawing a nude woman in Art. Ms Fossington-Gore said that it wasn't so much the subject matter but his ignorance of basic biological facts that was so upsetting. I did a good drawing of the Incredible Hulk smashing Craig Thomas to bits. Ms Fossington-Gore said it was a 'powerful statement of monolithic oppression'.

Phone call from my mother. Her voice sounded funny as if she had a cold. She kept saying, 'You'll understand one day, Adrian.' There was a slurping sound in the background. I expect it was that Lucas creep kissing her neck. I have seen them do it on the films.

Thursday, 12th September

It's the same every night now. Bombs and more bombs, and they're getting closer. A house got hit in Sandringham Road last night. That's one over from Summerfield. Sometimes I feel frightened and sometimes it makes me angry.

The Germans don't seem to care who they might kill. What's going through the minds of the pilots when they drop their bombs? Haven't they got wives and families? So how can they try to kill other people's children?

I mean, I understand why they might want to bomb a factory that's making guns. I can even understand why they might try to hit a power station. But what difference does it make to the war if they kill Mum, or Tom? Or me?

2) Working with a partner, write diary extracts for the day before and the day after each of the extracts above.

Assessment

SECTION 1

These final activities will give you an opportunity to assess children's all-round knowledge of *The Wreck of the Zanzibar*.

Assessment advice

The setting of Bryher is very important in *The Wreck of the Zanzibar*. The first assessment activity here will assess the children's overall knowledge of the setting, events and characters in the book. Completing photocopiable page 32 will give them an opportunity to locate key events and describe who was there, and what happened. The second activity concentrates on children's responses to individual diary entries. It looks in more depth at the way Michael Morpurgo builds up a picture of the island and the main characters. The third activity tests the children's knowledge of the book and one of its characters, but also encourages an imaginative response to the book.

Activity 1 – The big picture

Assessment focus: To demonstrate the children's knowledge of the structure of the story.
You will need: Photocopiable page 32.

- Hand out copies of photocopiable page 32, and ask children to do the following:
  - Mark on the map the names of the places where key events took place.
  - Make a note of what event happened in each place and write it on the map.
  - Write the names of the people involved and add them to the map.

Activity 2 – Getting up close

Assessment focus: To demonstrate the children's understanding of how the characters' actions are linked to events. To assess their awareness of how the natural setting of the island is reflected in the characters' attitudes and relationships.
You will need: Copies of the book, writing materials.

- Ask the children to choose two diary entries and write one or two paragraphs about the following:
  - What appeals to them in terms of the content (what happens in this entry).
  - The way the writer describes events (the language used to create the images of the actions and reactions of the characters).
  - How the writer links the island setting to events within the family.

Activity 3 – Taking it further

Assessment focus: To explore the children's imaginative response to the book.
You will need: Copies of the book, writing materials.

- Ask the children to imagine they are Billy as he sails away on the *General Lee*. He decides to write a letter to Laura, put it in a bottle and throw it over the side. He wants to explain the reasons for his actions. Ask the children to write Billy's message thinking about the following:
  - His reasons for leaving (the rows with Father, his frustration with having to look after the cows).
  - How he feels about Laura, his parents and Granny May (feelings of guilt because he has upset them).
  - His hopes and dreams (seeing the world; coming home full of tales, like Joseph Hannibal).

Assessment

SECTION 7

The big picture

1) Mark the place names that are mentioned in *The Wreck of the Zanzibar* on to this map.
2) Make a brief note of the events that happen in each place.
3) Write the names of the characters involved in each of these events.

N

PHOTOCOPIABLE

READ & RESPOND: Activities based on The Wreck of the Zanzibar

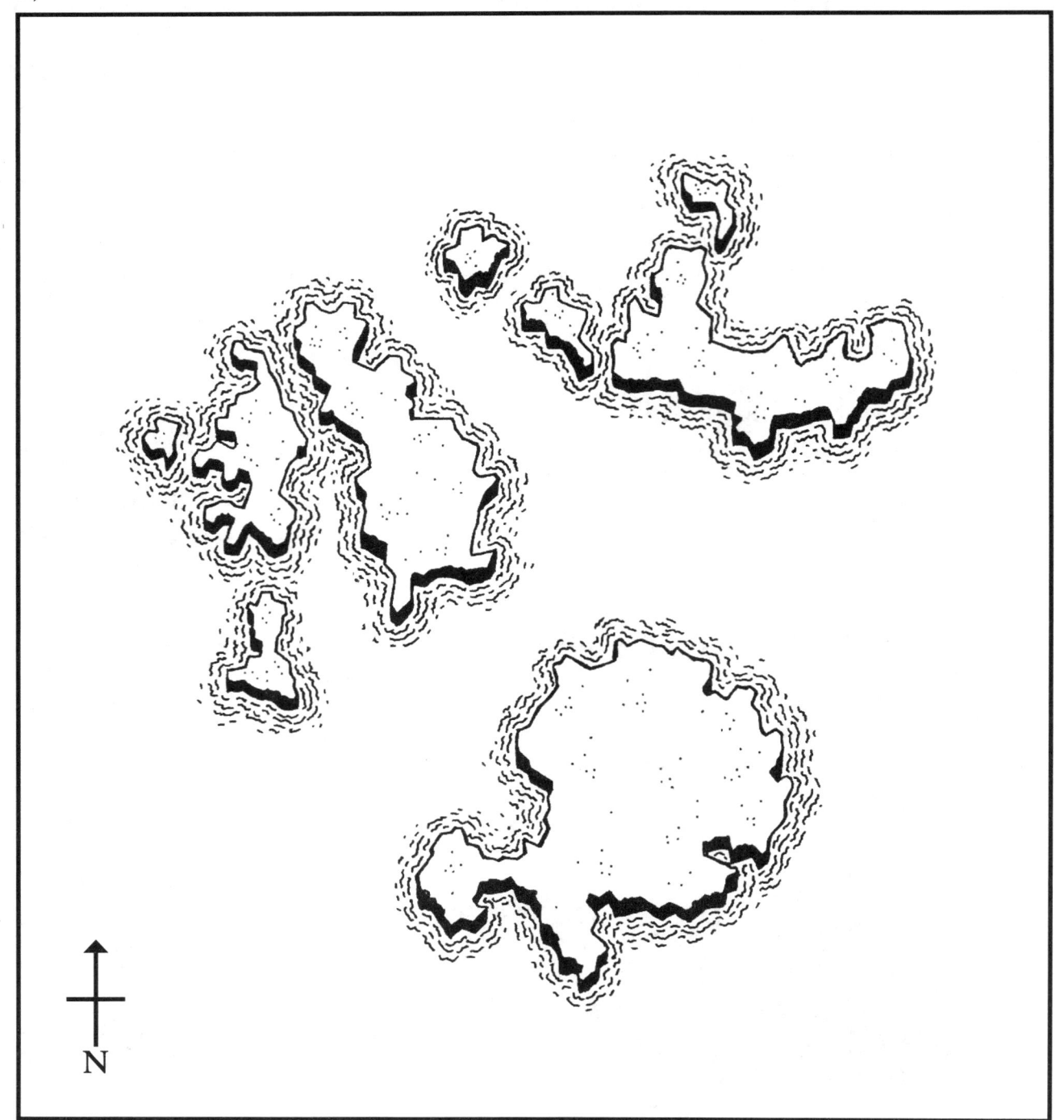

Illustration © The Drawing Room

SCHOLASTIC
www.scholastic.co.uk